Wedding Planner

Galison Books · New York

Contents

Calendar. 5-4

Budget. 41-6

Bridal Party. 63-7

Prenuptial Parties. 73-11

Ceremony. 119-12

Reception. 125-13

Guests. 131-15

Bridal Registry. 157-16

Honeymoon. 167-17

Notes. 173-17

CALENDAR

You require but a simple 'Yes'? Such a small word—but such an important one. But should not a heart so full of unutterable love as mine utter this little word with all it might? I do so and my innermost soul whispers always to you.

-CLARA WIECK TO ROBERT SCHUMANN, 18

Things to do at Least Six Months Ahead...

- ❏ Decide the type of wedding and approximate size.
- ❏ Morning, afternoon or evening?
- ❏ Set the date and time.
- ❏ Make a budget and discuss who will pay for what.
- ❏ Choose and reserve a place for the ceremony.
- ❏ Choose and reserve a location for the reception.
- ❏ Engage a judge or cleric to preside at the ceremony.
- ❏ Start compiling your guest list.
- ❏ Ask parents to begin to compile their guest lists.

Three to Six Months Ahead...

- [ ] Select a caterer.
- [ ] Set menu.
- [ ] Choose wines.
- [ ] Start researching bakers for wedding cakes.
- [ ] Hire musicians.
- [ ] Select a florist.
- [ ] Engage a photographer and/or videographer or crew.
- [ ] Choose a wedding dress or have one made.
- [ ] Select wedding party.
- [ ] Select and order bridesmaids' dresses.
- [ ] Finalize the look of the wedding and the color scheme.
- [ ] Finalize guest list.
- [ ] Order invitations and other stationery.
- [ ] Select lodging for out-of-town guests and make reservations.
- [ ] Select gifts for registry.
- [ ] Select honeymoon destination.
- [ ] Make honeymoon reservations.
- [ ] Select and reserve a location for the rehearsal dinner.

Six Months Ahead...

Five Months Ahead...

Four Months Ahead...

One to Three Months Ahead...

- ❑ Order the wedding cake.
- ❑ Give caterer and baker preliminary guest count.
- ❑ Arrange necessary rentals for reception.
- ❑ Discuss ceremony and vows with judge or cleric.
- ❑ Confirm dates and times with ceremony site and reception site management.
- ❑ Confirm dates and times with caterer, photographer, video cameraperson, musicians, florist, baker, and judge or cleric.
- ❑ Schedule formal wedding portrait, if having one.
- ❑ Plan menu for rehearsal dinner.
- ❑ Confirm date and time for rehearsal dinner.
- ❑ Schedule the wedding rehearsal.
- ❑ Discuss color scheme with bride's and groom's mothers so they can select their dresses.
- ❑ Fitting for wedding dress.
- ❑ Arrange fittings for bridesmaids.
- ❑ Select groom's attire.
- ❑ Select groomsmen's attire.
- ❑ Discuss attire with flower girl's and ring-bearer's parents.
- ❑ Select bridal shoes.
- ❑ Select and order wedding rings.

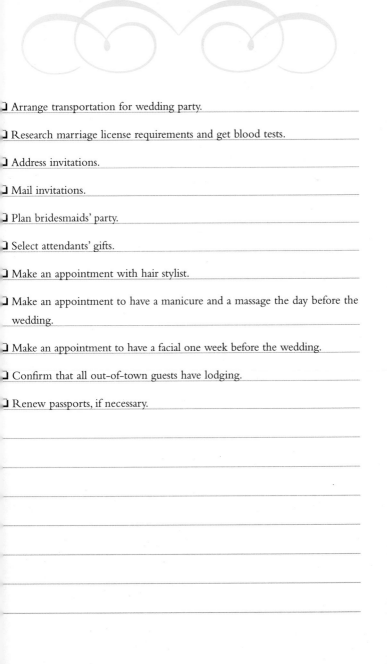

- ❏ Arrange transportation for wedding party.
- ❏ Research marriage license requirements and get blood tests.
- ❏ Address invitations.
- ❏ Mail invitations.
- ❏ Plan bridesmaids' party.
- ❏ Select attendants' gifts.
- ❏ Make an appointment with hair stylist.
- ❏ Make an appointment to have a manicure and a massage the day before the wedding.
- ❏ Make an appointment to have a facial one week before the wedding.
- ❏ Confirm that all out-of-town guests have lodging.
- ❏ Renew passports, if necessary.

Twelve Weeks Ahead...

Monday:

Tuesday:

Wednesday:

Thursday:

Friday:

Saturday:

Sunday:

Eleven Weeks Ahead...

Monday:

Tuesday:

Wednesday:

Thursday:

Friday:

Saturday:

Sunday:

Ten Weeks Ahead...

Monday:

Tuesday:

Wednesday:

Thursday:

Friday:

Saturday:

Sunday:

Nine Weeks Ahead...

Monday:

Tuesday:

Wednesday:

Thursday:

Friday:

Saturday:

Sunday:

Eight Weeks Ahead...

Monday:

Tuesday:

Wednesday:

Thursday:

Friday:

Saturday:

Sunday:

Seven Weeks Ahead...

Monday:

Tuesday:

Wednesday:

Thursday:

Friday:

Saturday:

Sunday:

Six Weeks Ahead...

Monday:

Tuesday:

Wednesday:

Thursday:

Friday:

Saturday:

Sunday:

Five Weeks Ahead...

Monday:

Tuesday:

Wednesday:

Thursday:

Friday:

Saturday:

Sunday:

One Month Ahead...

- ❏ Confirm guest count.
- ❏ Give caterer and baker guest count.
- ❏ Make seating chart and place cards for reception, if necessary.
- ❏ Make seating chart and place cards for rehearsal dinner, if necessary.
- ❏ Discuss musical selections with musicians.
- ❏ Purchase wine.
- ❏ Obtain marriage license.
- ❏ Write announcement for newspaper.
- ❏ Send wedding portrait and announcement to newspaper.
- ❏ Select "props" for ring-bearer and flower-girl (pillow, basket, etc.)
- ❏ Shop for clothes for honeymoon, if necessary.
- ❏ Wrap gifts for wedding party.

Four Weeks Ahead...

Monday:

Tuesday:

Wednesday:

Thursday:

Friday:

Saturday/Sunday:

Three Weeks Ahead…

Monday:

Tuesday:

Wednesday:

Thursday:

Friday:

Saturday/Sunday:

Two Weeks Ahead...

Monday:

Tuesday:

Wednesday:

Thursday:

Friday:

Saturday/Sunday:

One Week Ahead...

- ❑ Finalize guest count, give to caterer and baker.
- ❑ Reconfirm musicians and florist.
- ❑ Reconfirm photographer and/or videographer, and discuss particular shots you'll want.
- ❑ Have a facial.
- ❑ Pack for honeymoon.
- ❑ Try on wedding dress again in case of last-minute alterations.
- ❑ Call members of the wedding party to reconfirm rehearsal.

Seven Days Ahead...

Six Days Ahead...

Five Days Ahead...

Four Days Ahead…

Three Days Ahead…

The Day Before...

- ❏ Reconfirm airline flight.
- ❏ Manicure and massage.

Notes

BUDGET

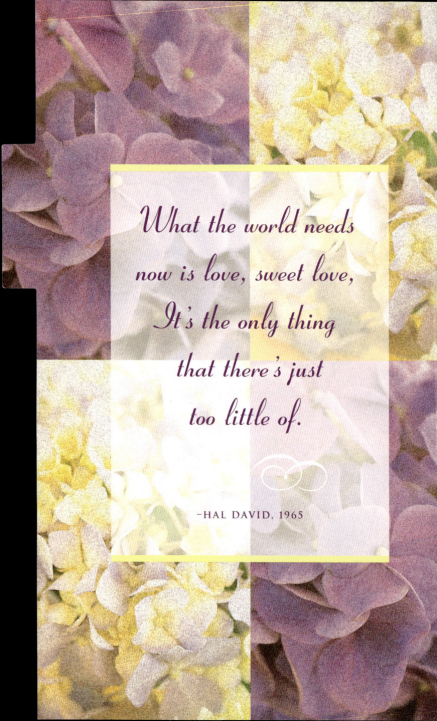

Budget

	Estimate	Actual
Ceremony Location		
Judge or Cleric's Fee		
Reception Location		
Caterer		
Wine, Champagne, etc.		
Wedding Cake		
Music, Ceremony		
Music, Reception		
Flowers, Ceremony		
Flowers, Wedding Party		
Flowers, Reception		
Other Decor		
Photography, Formal		
Photography, Ceremony		
Photography, Reception		
Videography		
Rentals		
Rehearsal Dinner		
Wedding Invitations		
Other Stationery		

Budget

	Estimate	Actual
Postage		
Accommodations		
Transportation		
Marriage License		
Blood Tests		
Bride's Dress		
Bridal Shoes		
Accessories		
Groom's Attire		
Wedding Rings		
Wedding Party Gifts		
Other:		

Budget

	Estimate	Actual
Other:		

Bakers

Baker:

Address:

Phone/fax:

Referred by:

Date called:

Estimate:

Notes:

Baker:

Address:

Phone/fax:

Referred by:

Date called:

Estimate:

Notes:

Baker:

Address:

Phone/fax:

Referred by:

Date called:

Estimate:

Notes:

Caterers

Caterer:

Address:

Phone/fax:

Referred by:

Date called:

Estimate:

Notes:

Caterer:

Address:

Phone/fax:

Referred by:

Date called:

Estimate:

Notes:

Caterer:

Address:

Phone/fax:

Referred by:

Date called:

Estimate:

Notes:

Wine

Liquor Store:

Address:

Phone/fax:

Referred by:

Date called:

Estimate:

Notes:

Liquor Store:

Address:

Phone/fax:

Referred by:

Date called:

Estimate:

Notes:

Liquor Store:

Address:

Phone/fax:

Referred by:

Date called:

Estimate:

Notes:

Music

Band Leader:

Address:

Phone/fax:

Referred by:

Date called:

Estimate:

Notes:

Band Leader:

Address:

Phone/fax:

Referred by:

Date called:

Estimate:

Notes:

Band Leader:

Address:

Phone/fax:

Referred by:

Date called:

Estimate:

Notes:

Photography

Photographer:

Address:

Phone/fax:

Referred by:

Date called:

Estimate:

Notes:

Photographer:

Address:

Phone/fax:

Referred by:

Date called:

Estimate:

Notes:

Photographer:

Address:

Phone/fax:

Referred by:

Date called:

Estimate:

Notes:

Videography

Videographer:

Address:

Phone/fax:

Referred by:

Date called:

Estimate:

Notes:

Videographer:

Address:

Phone/fax:

Referred by:

Date called:

Estimate:

Notes:

Videographer:

Address:

Phone/fax:

Referred by:

Date called:

Estimate:

Notes:

Rentals

Rental Company:

Address:

Phone/fax:

Referred by:

Date called:

Estimate:

Notes:

Rental Company:

Address:

Phone/fax:

Referred by:

Date called:

Estimate:

Notes:

Rental Company:

Address:

Phone/fax:

Referred by:

Date called:

Estimate:

Notes:

Transportation

Limousine Company:

Address:

Phone/fax:

Referred by:

Date called:

Estimate:

Notes:

Limousine Company:

Address:

Phone/fax:

Referred by:

Date called:

Estimate:

Notes:

Limousine Company:

Address:

Phone/fax:

Referred by:

Date called:

Estimate:

Notes:

Florists

Florist:

Address:

Phone/fax:

Referred by:

Date called:

Estimate:

Notes:

Florist:

Address:

Phone/fax:

Referred by:

Date called:

Estimate:

Notes:

Florist:

Address:

Phone/fax:

Referred by:

Date called:

Estimate:

Notes:

Wedding Dress

Bridal Shop: _____

Address: _____

Phone/fax: _____

Referred by: _____

Date called: _____

Estimate: _____

Notes: _____

_____

Bridal Shop: _____

Address: _____

Phone/fax: _____

Referred by: _____

Date called: _____

Estimate: _____

Notes: _____

_____

Bridal Shop: _____

Address: _____

Phone/fax: _____

Referred by: _____

Date called: _____

Estimate: _____

Notes: _____

_____

Final Suppliers

Baker:

Address:

Phone/fax:

Referred by:

Estimate:

Final cost:

Deposit due:

Reconfirmed:

Contract Signed:

Notes:

Caterer:

Address:

Phone/fax:

Referred by:

Estimate:

Final cost:

Deposit due:

Reconfirmed:

Contract Signed:

Notes:

Wine Store:

Address:

Phone/fax:

Referred by:

Estimate:

Final cost:

Deposit due:

Reconfirmed:

Contract Signed:

Notes:

Music:

Address:

Phone/fax:

Referred by:

Estimate:

Final cost:

Deposit due:

Reconfirmed:

Contract Signed:

Notes:

Photographer: _____

Address: _____

_____

Phone/fax: _____

Referred by: _____

Estimate: _____

Final cost: _____

Deposit due: _____

Reconfirmed: _____

Contract Signed: _____

Notes: _____

_____

Videographer: _____

Address: _____

_____

Phone/fax: _____

Referred by: _____

Estimate: _____

Final cost: _____

Deposit due: _____

Reconfirmed: _____

Contract Signed: _____

Notes: _____

_____

Rentals: _____

Address: _____

_____

Phone/fax: _____

Referred by: _____

Estimate: _____

Final cost: _____

Deposit due: _____

Reconfirmed: _____

Contract Signed: _____

Notes: _____

_____

Transportation: _____

Address: _____

_____

Phone/fax: _____

Referred by: _____

Estimate: _____

Final cost: _____

Deposit due: _____

Reconfirmed: _____

Contract Signed: _____

Notes: _____

_____

Florist:

Address:

Phone/fax:

Referred by:

Estimate:

Final cost:

Deposit due:

Reconfirmed:

Contract Signed:

Notes:

Wedding Dress:

Address:

Phone/fax:

Referred by:

Estimate:

Final cost:

Deposit due:

Reconfirmed:

Contract Signed:

Notes:

Other: _____

Address: _____

_____

Phone/fax: _____

Referred by: _____

Estimate: _____

Final cost: _____

Deposit due: _____

Reconfirmed: _____

Contract Signed: _____

Notes: _____

_____

Other: _____

Address: _____

_____

Phone/fax: _____

Referred by: _____

Estimate: _____

Final cost: _____

Deposit due: _____

Reconfirmed: _____

Contract Signed: _____

Notes: _____

_____

Other: _____

Address: _____

_____

Phone/fax: _____

Referred by: _____

Estimate: _____

Final cost: _____

Deposit due: _____

Reconfirmed: _____

Contract Signed: _____

Notes: _____

_____

Other: _____

Address: _____

_____

Phone/fax: _____

Referred by: _____

Estimate: _____

Final cost: _____

Deposit due: _____

Reconfirmed: _____

Contract Signed: _____

Notes: _____

_____

PRENUPTIAL
PARTIES

Oh, God!...for two days,

I have been asking myself every

moment if such happiness is not

a dream. It seems to me that

what I feel is not of earth.

I cannot yet comprehend this

cloudless heaven.

—VICTOR HUGO
TO ADÈLE FOUCHER, HIS FUTURE WIFE, 1821

Engagement Party

Hosted by:

Date:

Location:

Menu:

Notes:

ENGAGEMENT PARTY

Guests

Guest:

Address:

Phone:

Gift: Thank you sent:

Guest:

Address:

Phone:

Gift: Thank you sent:

Guest:

Address:

Phone:

Gift: Thank you sent:

Guest:

Address:

Phone:

Gift: Thank you sent:

Guest:

Address:

Phone:

Gift: Thank you sent:

Guest:

Address:

Phone:

Gift: Thank you sent:

Guests

Guest:

Address:

Phone:

Gift: Thank you sent:

Guest:

Address:

Phone:

Gift: Thank you sent:

Guest:

Address:

Phone:

Gift: Thank you sent:

Guest:

Address:

Phone:

Gift: Thank you sent:

Guest:

Address:

Phone:

Gift: Thank you sent:

Guest:

Address:

Phone:

Gift: Thank you sent:

Engagement Party Guests

Guest: _____
Address: _____
Phone: _____
Gift: _____ Thank you sent: _____

Guest: _____
Address: _____
Phone: _____
Gift: _____ Thank you sent: _____

Guest: _____
Address: _____
Phone: _____
Gift: _____ Thank you sent: _____

Guest: _____
Address: _____
Phone: _____
Gift: _____ Thank you sent: _____

Guest: _____
Address: _____
Phone: _____
Gift: _____ Thank you sent: _____

Guest: _____
Address: _____
Phone: _____
Gift: _____ Thank you sent: _____

Guests

Guest:

Address:

Phone:

Gift: Thank you sent:

Guest:

Address:

Phone:

Gift: Thank you sent:

Guest:

Address:

Phone:

Gift: Thank you sent:

Guest:

Address:

Phone:

Gift: Thank you sent:

Guest:

Address:

Phone:

Gift: Thank you sent:

Guest:

Address:

Phone:

Gift: Thank you sent:

ENGAGEMENT PARTY

Guests

Guest:

Address:

Phone:

Gift: Thank you sent:

Guest:

Address:

Phone:

Gift: Thank you sent:

Guest:

Address:

Phone:

Gift: Thank you sent:

Guest:

Address:

Phone:

Gift: Thank you sent:

Guest:

Address:

Phone:

Gift: Thank you sent:

Guest:

Address:

Phone:

Gift: Thank you sent:

Guests

Guest:

Address:

Phone:

Gift: Thank you sent:

Guest:

Address:

Phone:

Gift: Thank you sent:

Guest:

Address:

Phone:

Gift: Thank you sent:

Guest:

Address:

Phone:

Gift: Thank you sent:

Guest:

Address:

Phone:

Gift: Thank you sent:

Guest:

Address:

Phone:

Gift: Thank you sent:

Engagement Party

Guests

Guest:

Address:

Phone:

Gift: Thank you sent:

Guest:

Address:

Phone:

Gift: Thank you sent:

Guest:

Address:

Phone:

Gift: Thank you sent:

Guest:

Address:

Phone:

Gift: Thank you sent:

Guest:

Address:

Phone:

Gift: Thank you sent:

Guest:

Address:

Phone:

Gift: Thank you sent:

Guests

Guest:

Address:

Phone:

Gift: Thank you sent:

Guest:

Address:

Phone:

Gift: Thank you sent:

Guest:

Address:

Phone:

Gift: Thank you sent:

Guest:

Address:

Phone:

Gift: Thank you sent:

Guest:

Address:

Phone:

Gift: Thank you sent:

Guest:

Address:

Phone:

Gift: Thank you sent:

Engagement Party Guests

Guest:

Address:

Phone:

Gift: Thank you sent:

Guest:

Address:

Phone:

Gift: Thank you sent:

Guest:

Address:

Phone:

Gift: Thank you sent:

Guest:

Address:

Phone:

Gift: Thank you sent:

Guest:

Address:

Phone:

Gift: Thank you sent:

Guest:

Address:

Phone:

Gift: Thank you sent:

Guests

Guest:

Address:

Phone:

Gift: Thank you sent:

Guest:

Address:

Phone:

Gift: Thank you sent:

Guest:

Address:

Phone:

Gift: Thank you sent:

Guest:

Address:

Phone:

Gift: Thank you sent:

Guest:

Address:

Phone:

Gift: Thank you sent:

Guest:

Address:

Phone:

Gift: Thank you sent:

ENGAGEMENT PARTY

Guests

Guest:
Address:
Phone:
Gift: Thank you sent:

Guest:
Address:
Phone:
Gift: Thank you sent:

Guest:
Address:
Phone:
Gift: Thank you sent:

Guest:
Address:
Phone:
Gift: Thank you sent:

Guest:
Address:
Phone:
Gift: Thank you sent:

Guest:
Address:
Phone:
Gift: Thank you sent:

Guests

Guest:

Address:

Phone:

Gift: Thank you sent:

Guest:

Address:

Phone:

Gift: Thank you sent:

Guest:

Address:

Phone:

Gift: Thank you sent:

Guest:

Address:

Phone:

Gift: Thank you sent:

Guest:

Address:

Phone:

Gift: Thank you sent:

Guest:

Address:

Phone:

Gift: Thank you sent:

# Engagement Party Guests

Guest: _____
Address: _____
Phone: _____
Gift: _____ Thank you sent: _____

Guest: _____
Address: _____
Phone: _____
Gift: _____ Thank you sent: _____

Guest: _____
Address: _____
Phone: _____
Gift: _____ Thank you sent: _____

Guest: _____
Address: _____
Phone: _____
Gift: _____ Thank you sent: _____

Guest: _____
Address: _____
Phone: _____
Gift: _____ Thank you sent: _____

Guest: _____
Address: _____
Phone: _____
Gift: _____ Thank you sent: _____

Guests

Guest:

Address:

Phone:

Gift: Thank you sent:

Guest:

Address:

Phone:

Gift: Thank you sent:

Guest:

Address:

Phone:

Gift: Thank you sent:

Guest:

Address:

Phone:

Gift: Thank you sent:

Guest:

Address:

Phone:

Gift: Thank you sent:

Guest:

Address:

Phone:

Gift: Thank you sent:

ENGAGEMENT PARTY

Guests

Guest:

Address:

Phone:

Gift:					Thank you sent:

Guest:

Address:

Phone:

Gift:					Thank you sent:

Guest:

Address:

Phone:

Gift:					Thank you sent:

Guest:

Address:

Phone:

Gift:					Thank you sent:

Guest:

Address:

Phone:

Gift:					Thank you sent:

Guest:

Address:

Phone:

Gift:					Thank you sent:

Guests

Guest:

Address:

Phone:

Gift: Thank you sent:

Guest:

Address:

Phone:

Gift: Thank you sent:

Guest:

Address:

Phone:

Gift: Thank you sent:

Guest:

Address:

Phone:

Gift: Thank you sent:

Guest:

Address:

Phone:

Gift: Thank you sent:

Guest:

Address:

Phone:

Gift: Thank you sent:

Bridal Shower

Hosted by:

Date:

Location:

Menu:

Theme:

Notes:

Guests

Guest:

Address:

Phone:

Gift: Thank you sent:

Guest:

Address:

Phone:

Gift: Thank you sent:

Guest:

Address:

Phone:

Gift: Thank you sent:

Guest:

Address:

Phone:

Gift: Thank you sent:

Guest:

Address:

Phone:

Gift: Thank you sent:

Guest:

Address:

Phone:

Gift: Thank you sent:

BRIDAL SHOWER

Guests

Guest: _____
Address: _____
Phone: _____
Gift: _____ Thank you sent: _____

Guest: _____
Address: _____
Phone: _____
Gift: _____ Thank you sent: _____

Guest: _____
Address: _____
Phone: _____
Gift: _____ Thank you sent: _____

Guest: _____
Address: _____
Phone: _____
Gift: _____ Thank you sent: _____

Guest: _____
Address: _____
Phone: _____
Gift: _____ Thank you sent: _____

Guest: _____
Address: _____
Phone: _____
Gift: _____ Thank you sent: _____

Guests

Guest:

Address:

Phone:

Gift: Thank you sent:

Guest:

Address:

Phone:

Gift: Thank you sent:

Guest:

Address:

Phone:

Gift: Thank you sent:

Guest:

Address:

Phone:

Gift: Thank you sent:

Guest:

Address:

Phone:

Gift: Thank you sent:

Guest:

Address:

Phone:

Gift: Thank you sent:

Bridal Shower

Guests

Guest:

Address:

Phone:

Gift: Thank you sent:

Guest:

Address:

Phone:

Gift: Thank you sent:

Guest:

Address:

Phone:

Gift: Thank you sent:

Guest:

Address:

Phone:

Gift: Thank you sent:

Guest:

Address:

Phone:

Gift: Thank you sent:

Guest:

Address:

Phone:

Gift: Thank you sent:

Guests

Guest:

Address:

Phone:

Gift: Thank you sent:

Guest:

Address:

Phone:

Gift: Thank you sent:

Guest:

Address:

Phone:

Gift: Thank you sent:

Guest:

Address:

Phone:

Gift: Thank you sent:

Guest:

Address:

Phone:

Gift: Thank you sent:

Guest:

Address:

Phone:

Gift: Thank you sent:

Bridal Shower

Hosted by: _____

Date: _____

Location: _____

Menu: _____
_____
_____
_____
_____
_____

Theme: _____
_____
_____

Notes: _____
_____
_____
_____
_____
_____
_____
_____
_____
_____
_____
_____

Guests

Guest:

Address:

Phone:

Gift: Thank you sent:

Guest:

Address:

Phone:

Gift: Thank you sent:

Guest:

Address:

Phone:

Gift: Thank you sent:

Guest:

Address:

Phone:

Gift: Thank you sent:

Guest:

Address:

Phone:

Gift: Thank you sent:

Guest:

Address:

Phone:

Gift: Thank you sent:

Bridal Shower Guests

Guest:
Address:
Phone:
Gift: Thank you sent:

Guest:
Address:
Phone:
Gift: Thank you sent:

Guest:
Address:
Phone:
Gift: Thank you sent:

Guest:
Address:
Phone:
Gift: Thank you sent:

Guest:
Address:
Phone:
Gift: Thank you sent:

Guest:
Address:
Phone:
Gift: Thank you sent:

Guests

Guest:

Address:

Phone:

Gift: Thank you sent:

Guest:

Address:

Phone:

Gift: Thank you sent:

Guest:

Address:

Phone:

Gift: Thank you sent:

Guest:

Address:

Phone:

Gift: Thank you sent:

Guest:

Address:

Phone:

Gift: Thank you sent:

Guest:

Address:

Phone:

Gift: Thank you sent:

Bridal Shower Guests

Guest:

Address:

Phone:

Gift: Thank you sent:

Guest:

Address:

Phone:

Gift: Thank you sent:

Guest:

Address:

Phone:

Gift: Thank you sent:

Guest:

Address:

Phone:

Gift: Thank you sent:

Guest:

Address:

Phone:

Gift: Thank you sent:

Guest:

Address:

Phone:

Gift: Thank you sent:

Guests

Guest:

Address:

Phone:

Gift: Thank you sent:

Guest:

Address:

Phone:

Gift: Thank you sent:

Guest:

Address:

Phone:

Gift: Thank you sent:

Guest:

Address:

Phone:

Gift: Thank you sent:

Guest:

Address:

Phone:

Gift: Thank you sent:

Guest:

Address:

Phone:

Gift: Thank you sent:

Bridesmaids' Party

Hosted by:

Date:

Location:

Menu:

Gift for maid/matron of honor:

Gift for bridesmaids:

Notes:

Guests

Guest:

Address:

Phone:

RSVP:

Guest:

Address:

Phone:

RSVP:

Guest:

Address:

Phone:

RSVP:

Guest:

Address:

Phone:

RSVP:

Guest:

Address:

Phone:

RSVP:

Guest:

Address:

Phone:

RSVP:

Bridesmaids' Party

Guests

Guest: _____

Address: _____

Phone: _____

RSVP: _____

Guest: _____

Address: _____

Phone: _____

RSVP: _____

Guest: _____

Address: _____

Phone: _____

RSVP: _____

Guest: _____

Address: _____

Phone: _____

RSVP: _____

Guest: _____

Address: _____

Phone: _____

RSVP: _____

Guest: _____

Address: _____

Phone: _____

RSVP: _____

Guests

Guest:

Address:

Phone:

RSVP:

Guest:

Address:

Phone:

RSVP:

Guest:

Address:

Phone:

RSVP:

Guest:

Address:

Phone:

RSVP:

Guest:

Address:

Phone:

RSVP:

Guest:

Address:

Phone:

RSVP:

Bachelors Party

Hosted by:

Date:

Location:

Menu:

Gift for best man:

Gifts for ushers:

Notes:

Guests

Guest:

Address:

Phone:

RSVP:

Guest:

Address:

Phone:

RSVP:

Guest:

Address:

Phone:

RSVP:

Guest:

Address:

Phone:

RSVP:

Guest:

Address:

Phone:

RSVP:

Guest:

Address:

Phone:

RSVP:

Bachelor Party

Guests

Guest: _____

Address: _____

Phone: _____

RSVP: _____

Guest: _____

Address: _____

Phone: _____

RSVP: _____

Guest: _____

Address: _____

Phone: _____

RSVP: _____

Guest: _____

Address: _____

Phone: _____

RSVP: _____

Guest: _____

Address: _____

Phone: _____

RSVP: _____

Guest: _____

Address: _____

Phone: _____

RSVP: _____

Guests

Guest:

Address:

Phone:

RSVP:

Guest:

Address:

Phone:

RSVP:

Guest:

Address:

Phone:

RSVP:

Guest:

Address:

Phone:

RSVP:

Guest:

Address:

Phone:

RSVP:

Guest:

Address:

Phone:

RSVP:

Rehearsal Dinner

Hosted by:

Date:

Location:

Total Attending:

Menu:

Notes:

Seating Chart

Sketch your table arrangements and seating chart below:

Rehearsal Dinner Guests

Guest:

Address:

Phone:

R.S.V.P.: Number attending:

Guest:

Address:

Phone:

R.S.V.P.: Number attending:

Guest:

Address:

Phone:

R.S.V.P.: Number attending:

Guest:

Address:

Phone:

R.S.V.P.: Number attending:

Guest:

Address:

Phone:

R.S.V.P.: Number attending:

Guest:

Address:

Phone:

R.S.V.P.: Number attending:

Guests

Guest: _____

Address: _____

Phone: _____

R.S.V.P.: _____ Number attending: _____

Guest: _____

Address: _____

Phone: _____

R.S.V.P.: _____ Number attending: _____

Guest: _____

Address: _____

Phone: _____

R.S.V.P.: _____ Number attending: _____

Guest: _____

Address: _____

Phone: _____

R.S.V.P.: _____ Number attending: _____

Guest: _____

Address: _____

Phone: _____

R.S.V.P.: _____ Number attending: _____

Guest: _____

Address: _____

Phone: _____

R.S.V.P.: _____ Number attending: _____

Rehearsal Dinner Guests

Guest:

Address:

Phone:

R.S.V.P.:   Number attending:

Guest:

Address:

Phone:

R.S.V.P.:   Number attending:

Guest:

Address:

Phone:

R.S.V.P.:   Number attending:

Guest:

Address:

Phone:

R.S.V.P.:   Number attending:

Guest:

Address:

Phone:

R.S.V.P.:   Number attending:

Guest:

Address:

Phone:

R.S.V.P.:   Number attending:

Guests

Guest:

Address:

Phone:

R.S.V.P.:   Number attending:

Guest:

Address:

Phone:

R.S.V.P.:   Number attending:

Guest:

Address:

Phone:

R.S.V.P.:   Number attending:

Guest:

Address:

Phone:

R.S.V.P.:   Number attending:

Guest:

Address:

Phone:

R.S.V.P.:   Number attending:

Guest:

Address:

Phone:

R.S.V.P.:   Number attending:

Rehearsal Dinner Guests

Guest:

Address:

Phone:

R.S.V.P.: Number attending:

Guest:

Address:

Phone:

R.S.V.P.: Number attending:

Guest:

Address:

Phone:

R.S.V.P.: Number attending:

Guest:

Address:

Phone:

R.S.V.P.: Number attending:

Guest:

Address:

Phone:

R.S.V.P.: Number attending:

Guest:

Address:

Phone:

R.S.V.P.: Number attending:

Guests

Guest: _____

Address: _____

Phone: _____

R.S.V.P.: _____ Number attending: _____

Guest: _____

Address: _____

Phone: _____

R.S.V.P.: _____ Number attending: _____

Guest: _____

Address: _____

Phone: _____

R.S.V.P.: _____ Number attending: _____

Guest: _____

Address: _____

Phone: _____

R.S.V.P.: _____ Number attending: _____

Guest: _____

Address: _____

Phone: _____

R.S.V.P.: _____ Number attending: _____

Guest: _____

Address: _____

Phone: _____

R.S.V.P.: _____ Number attending: _____

Rehearsal Dinner Guests

Guest:

Address:

Phone:

R.S.V.P.:   Number attending:

Guest:

Address:

Phone:

R.S.V.P.:   Number attending:

Guest:

Address:

Phone:

R.S.V.P.:   Number attending:

Guest:

Address:

Phone:

R.S.V.P.:   Number attending:

Guest:

Address:

Phone:

R.S.V.P.:   Number attending:

Guest:

Address:

Phone:

R.S.V.P.:   Number attending:

BRIDAL/PARTY

*If love were what
the rose is,
And I were like the leaf,
Our lives would grow
together in sad or
singing weather.*

—ALGERNON CHARLES SWINBURNE
A MATCH, 1866

Bridal Party

Maid/Matron of Honor:

Address:

Home phone

Work phone/fax:

Dress size:

Color:

Shoe size:

Measurements:

Notes:

Best Man:

Address:

Phone/fax:

Measurements:

Jacket size:

Shirt: Sleeve:

Waist: Inseam:

Outseam:

Shoe size:

Notes:

Bridal Party

Flower Girl: _____

Parent _____

Address: _____

Phone: _____

Measurements: _____

Notes: _____

_____

_____

Ring Bearer: _____

Parent: _____

Address: _____

Phone: _____

Measurements: _____

Notes: _____

_____

_____

Bride's Mother: _____

Style & Length: _____

Color: _____

Measurements: _____

Accessories: _____

Notes: _____

_____

_____

Groom's Mother: _____

Style & Length: _____

Color: _____

Measurements: _____

Accessories: _____

Notes: _____
_____
_____

Bride's Father: _____

Suit Style & Color: _____

Measurements: _____
_____

Tie Color: _____

Notes: _____
_____
_____

Groom's Father: _____

Suit Style & Color: _____

Measurements: _____
_____

Tie Color: _____

Notes: _____
_____
_____

Bridesmaids

Bridesmaid: _____

Address: _____

Home phone _____

Work phone/fax: _____

Dress size: _____ Shoe size: _____

Measurements: _____

Notes: _____

Bridesmaid: _____

Address: _____

Home phone _____

Work phone/fax: _____

Dress size: _____ Shoe size: _____

Measurements: _____

Notes: _____

Bridesmaid: _____

Address: _____

Home phone _____

Work phone/fax: _____

Dress size: _____ Shoe size: _____

Measurements: _____

Notes: _____

Bridesmaid:

Address:

Home phone

Work phone/fax:

Dress size: Shoe size:

Measurements:

Notes:

Bridesmaid:

Address:

Home phone

Work phone/fax:

Dress size: Shoe size:

Measurements:

Notes:

Bridesmaid:

Address:

Home phone

Work phone/fax:

Dress size: Shoe size:

Measurements:

Notes:

Bridesmaid:

Address:

Home phone

Work phone/fax:

Dress size: Shoe size:

Measurements:

Notes:

Bridesmaid:

Address:

Home phone

Work phone/fax:

Dress size: Shoe size:

Measurements:

Notes:

Bridesmaid:

Address:

Home phone

Work phone/fax:

Dress size: Shoe size:

Measurements:

Notes:

Bridesmaid:

Address:

Home phone

Work phone/fax:

Dress size: Shoe size:

Measurements:

Notes:

Bridesmaid:

Address:

Home phone

Work phone/fax:

Dress size: Shoe size:

Measurements:

Notes:

Bridesmaid:

Address:

Home phone

Work phone/fax:

Dress size: Shoe size:

Measurements:

Notes:

Ushers

Usher:

Address:

Phone/fax:

Measurements: Jacket size:

Shirt: Sleeve: Waist:

Inseam: Outseam: Shoe size:

Notes:

Usher:

Address:

Phone/fax:

Measurements: Jacket size:

Shirt: Sleeve: Waist:

Inseam: Outseam: Shoe size:

Notes:

Usher:

Address:

Phone/fax:

Measurements: Jacket size:

Shirt: Sleeve: Waist:

Inseam: Outseam: Shoe size:

Notes:

Usher:

Address:

Phone/fax:

Measurements: Jacket size:

Shirt: Sleeve: Waist:

Inseam: Outseam: Shoe size:

Notes:

Usher:

Address:

Phone/fax:

Measurements: Jacket size:

Shirt: Sleeve: Waist:

Inseam: Outseam: Shoe size:

Notes:

Usher:

Address:

Phone/fax:

Measurements: Jacket size:

Shirt: Sleeve: Waist:

Inseam: Outseam: Shoe size:

Notes:

Usher:

Address:

Phone/fax:

Measurements: Jacket size:

Shirt: Sleeve: Waist:

Inseam: Outseam: Shoe size:

Notes:

Usher:

Address:

Phone/fax:

Measurements: Jacket size:

Shirt: Sleeve: Waist:

Inseam: Outseam: Shoe size:

Notes:

Usher:

Address:

Phone/fax:

Measurements: Jacket size:

Shirt: Sleeve: Waist:

Inseam: Outseam: Shoe size:

Notes:

CEREMONY

Daisy, Daisy, give me your answer do!

I'm half crazy, all for the love of you!

It won't be a stylish marriage,

I can't afford a carriage,

But you'll look sweet upon the seat

Of a bicycle built for two!

—HARRY DACRE, 18

Ceremony

Location:

Address:

Phone/fax:

Time:

Officiants:

Music:

Schedule:

Vows/Readings:

Ceremony

Processional:

Recessional:

Transportation to reception:

Notes:

Notes

RECEPTION

Originally, the newly married couple saved the top tier of the wedding cake for the arrival of their first child—usually about a year after the wedding. The tradition evolved into freezing the top tier and eating it on the first wedding anniversary.

Reception

Location: _____

Address: _____

_____

Time: _____

Contract Signed: _____

Music: _____

_____

_____

_____

_____

_____

_____

Menu: _____

_____

_____

_____

_____

_____

_____

_____

_____

_____

Decor:

Toasts:

Seating Chart

Sketch your table arrangements and seating chart below:

Seating Chart

Notes

GUESTS

> Neither a lofty
> degree of intelligence
> nor imagination
> nor both together go to
> the making of genius.
> Love, love, love,
> that is the soul of genius.
>
> —WOLFGANG AMADÈ MOZART

Guests

Guest:

Address:

Phone:

R.S.V.P.: Number attending:

Gift: Thank you sent:

Guest:

Address:

Phone:

R.S.V.P.: Number attending:

Gift: Thank you sent:

Guest:

Address:

Phone:

R.S.V.P.: Number attending:

Gift: Thank you sent:

Guest:

Address:

Phone:

R.S.V.P.: Number attending:

Gift: Thank you sent:

Guest:

Address:

Phone:

R.S.V.P.: Number attending:

Gift: Thank you sent:

RECEPTION

Guests

Guest:

Address:

Phone:

R.S.V.P.: Number attending:

Gift: Thank you sent:

Guest:

Address:

Phone:

R.S.V.P.: Number attending:

Gift: Thank you sent:

Guest:

Address:

Phone:

R.S.V.P.: Number attending:

Gift: Thank you sent:

Guest:

Address:

Phone:

R.S.V.P.: Number attending:

Gift: Thank you sent:

Guest:

Address:

Phone:

R.S.V.P.: Number attending:

Gift: Thank you sent:

Guests

Guest:

Address:

Phone:

R.S.V.P.: Number attending:

Gift: Thank you sent:

Guest:

Address:

Phone:

R.S.V.P.: Number attending:

Gift: Thank you sent:

Guest:

Address:

Phone:

R.S.V.P.: Number attending:

Gift: Thank you sent:

Guest:

Address:

Phone:

R.S.V.P.: Number attending:

Gift: Thank you sent:

Guest:

Address:

Phone:

R.S.V.P.: Number attending:

Gift: Thank you sent:

RECEPTION

Guests

Guest:

Address:

Phone:

R.S.V.P.: Number attending:

Gift: Thank you sent:

Guest:

Address:

Phone:

R.S.V.P.: Number attending:

Gift: Thank you sent:

Guest:

Address:

Phone:

R.S.V.P.: Number attending:

Gift: Thank you sent:

Guest:

Address:

Phone:

R.S.V.P.: Number attending:

Gift: Thank you sent:

Guest:

Address:

Phone:

R.S.V.P.: Number attending:

Gift: Thank you sent:

Guests

Guest:

Address:

Phone:

R.S.V.P.: Number attending:

Gift: Thank you sent:

Guest:

Address:

Phone:

R.S.V.P.: Number attending:

Gift: Thank you sent:

Guest:

Address:

Phone:

R.S.V.P.: Number attending:

Gift: Thank you sent:

Guest:

Address:

Phone:

R.S.V.P.: Number attending:

Gift: Thank you sent:

Guest:

Address:

Phone:

R.S.V.P.: Number attending:

Gift: Thank you sent:

RECEPTION

Guests

Guest: _____

Address: _____

Phone: _____

R.S.V.P.: _____ Number attending: _____

Gift: _____ Thank you sent: _____

Guest: _____

Address: _____

Phone: _____

R.S.V.P.: _____ Number attending: _____

Gift: _____ Thank you sent: _____

Guest: _____

Address: _____

Phone: _____

R.S.V.P.: _____ Number attending: _____

Gift: _____ Thank you sent: _____

Guest: _____

Address: _____

Phone: _____

R.S.V.P.: _____ Number attending: _____

Gift: _____ Thank you sent: _____

Guest: _____

Address: _____

Phone: _____

R.S.V.P.: _____ Number attending: _____

Gift: _____ Thank you sent: _____

Guests

Guest:

Address:

Phone:

R.S.V.P.: Number attending:

Gift: Thank you sent:

Guest:

Address:

Phone:

R.S.V.P.: Number attending:

Gift: Thank you sent:

Guest:

Address:

Phone:

R.S.V.P.: Number attending:

Gift: Thank you sent:

Guest:

Address:

Phone:

R.S.V.P.: Number attending:

Gift: Thank you sent:

Guest:

Address:

Phone:

R.S.V.P.: Number attending:

Gift: Thank you sent:

RECEPTION

Guests

Guest: _____

Address: _____

Phone: _____

R.S.V.P.: _____ Number attending: _____

Gift: _____ Thank you sent: _____

Guest: _____

Address: _____

Phone: _____

R.S.V.P.: _____ Number attending: _____

Gift: _____ Thank you sent: _____

Guest: _____

Address: _____

Phone: _____

R.S.V.P.: _____ Number attending: _____

Gift: _____ Thank you sent: _____

Guest: _____

Address: _____

Phone: _____

R.S.V.P.: _____ Number attending: _____

Gift: _____ Thank you sent: _____

Guest: _____

Address: _____

Phone: _____

R.S.V.P.: _____ Number attending: _____

Gift: _____ Thank you sent: _____

Guests

Guest:

Address:

Phone:

R.S.V.P.: Number attending:

Gift: Thank you sent:

Guest:

Address:

Phone:

R.S.V.P.: Number attending:

Gift: Thank you sent:

Guest:

Address:

Phone:

R.S.V.P.: Number attending:

Gift: Thank you sent:

Guest:

Address:

Phone:

R.S.V.P.: Number attending:

Gift: Thank you sent:

Guest:

Address:

Phone:

R.S.V.P.: Number attending:

Gift: Thank you sent:

RECEPTION

Guests

Guest:

Address:

Phone:

R.S.V.P.: Number attending:

Gift: Thank you sent:

Guest:

Address:

Phone:

R.S.V.P.: Number attending:

Gift: Thank you sent:

Guest:

Address:

Phone:

R.S.V.P.: Number attending:

Gift: Thank you sent:

Guest:

Address:

Phone:

R.S.V.P.: Number attending:

Gift: Thank you sent:

Guest:

Address:

Phone:

R.S.V.P.: Number attending:

Gift: Thank you sent:

Guests

Guest:

Address:

Phone:

R.S.V.P.:   Number attending:

Gift: Thank you sent:

Guest:

Address:

Phone:

R.S.V.P.:   Number attending:

Gift: Thank you sent:

Guest:

Address:

Phone:

R.S.V.P.:   Number attending:

Gift: Thank you sent:

Guest:

Address:

Phone:

R.S.V.P.:   Number attending:

Gift: Thank you sent:

Guest:

Address:

Phone:

R.S.V.P.:   Number attending:

Gift: Thank you sent:

Reception

Guests

Guest:

Address:

Phone:

R.S.V.P.: Number attending:

Gift: Thank you sent:

Guest:

Address:

Phone:

R.S.V.P.: Number attending:

Gift: Thank you sent:

Guest:

Address:

Phone:

R.S.V.P.: Number attending:

Gift: Thank you sent:

Guest:

Address:

Phone:

R.S.V.P.: Number attending:

Gift: Thank you sent:

Guest:

Address:

Phone:

R.S.V.P.: Number attending:

Gift: Thank you sent:

Guests

Guest:

Address:

Phone:

R.S.V.P.: Number attending:

Gift: Thank you sent:

Guest:

Address:

Phone:

R.S.V.P.: Number attending:

Gift: Thank you sent:

Guest:

Address:

Phone:

R.S.V.P.: Number attending:

Gift: Thank you sent:

Guest:

Address:

Phone:

R.S.V.P.: Number attending:

Gift: Thank you sent:

Guest:

Address:

Phone:

R.S.V.P.: Number attending:

Gift: Thank you sent:

RECEPTION

Guests

Guest:

Address:

Phone:

R.S.V.P.: Number attending:

Gift: Thank you sent:

Guest:

Address:

Phone:

R.S.V.P.: Number attending:

Gift: Thank you sent:

Guest:

Address:

Phone:

R.S.V.P.: Number attending:

Gift: Thank you sent:

Guest:

Address:

Phone:

R.S.V.P.: Number attending:

Gift: Thank you sent:

Guest:

Address:

Phone:

R.S.V.P.: Number attending:

Gift: Thank you sent:

Guests

Guest:

Address:

Phone:

R.S.V.P.:   Number attending:

Gift: Thank you sent:

Guest:

Address:

Phone:

R.S.V.P.:   Number attending:

Gift: Thank you sent:

Guest:

Address:

Phone:

R.S.V.P.:   Number attending:

Gift: Thank you sent:

Guest:

Address:

Phone:

R.S.V.P.:   Number attending:

Gift: Thank you sent:

Guest:

Address:

Phone:

R.S.V.P.:   Number attending:

Gift: Thank you sent:

RECEPTION

Guests

Guest:

Address:

Phone:

R.S.V.P.:   Number attending:

Gift: Thank you sent:

Guest:

Address:

Phone:

R.S.V.P.:   Number attending:

Gift: Thank you sent:

Guest:

Address:

Phone:

R.S.V.P.:   Number attending:

Gift: Thank you sent:

Guest:

Address:

Phone:

R.S.V.P.:   Number attending:

Gift: Thank you sent:

Guest:

Address:

Phone:

R.S.V.P.:   Number attending:

Gift: Thank you sent:

Guests

Guest: _____

Address: _____

Phone: _____

R.S.V.P.: _____ Number attending: _____

Gift: _____ Thank you sent: _____

Guest: _____

Address: _____

Phone: _____

R.S.V.P.: _____ Number attending: _____

Gift: _____ Thank you sent: _____

Guest: _____

Address: _____

Phone: _____

R.S.V.P.: _____ Number attending: _____

Gift: _____ Thank you sent: _____

Guest: _____

Address: _____

Phone: _____

R.S.V.P.: _____ Number attending: _____

Gift: _____ Thank you sent: _____

Guest: _____

Address: _____

Phone: _____

R.S.V.P.: _____ Number attending: _____

Gift: _____ Thank you sent: _____

RECEPTION

Guests

Guest:

Address:

Phone:

R.S.V.P.:   Number attending:

Gift: Thank you sent:

Guest:

Address:

Phone:

R.S.V.P.:   Number attending:

Gift: Thank you sent:

Guest:

Address:

Phone:

R.S.V.P.:   Number attending:

Gift: Thank you sent:

Guest:

Address:

Phone:

R.S.V.P.:   Number attending:

Gift: Thank you sent:

Guest:

Address:

Phone:

R.S.V.P.:   Number attending:

Gift: Thank you sent:

Guests

Guest:

Address:

Phone:

R.S.V.P.: Number attending:

Gift: Thank you sent:

Guest:

Address:

Phone:

R.S.V.P.: Number attending:

Gift: Thank you sent:

Guest:

Address:

Phone:

R.S.V.P.: Number attending:

Gift: Thank you sent:

Guest:

Address:

Phone:

R.S.V.P.: Number attending:

Gift: Thank you sent:

Guest:

Address:

Phone:

R.S.V.P.: Number attending:

Gift: Thank you sent:

RECEPTION

Guests

Guest:

Address:

Phone:

R.S.V.P.: Number attending:

Gift: Thank you sent:

Guest:

Address:

Phone:

R.S.V.P.: Number attending:

Gift: Thank you sent:

Guest:

Address:

Phone:

R.S.V.P.: Number attending:

Gift: Thank you sent:

Guest:

Address:

Phone:

R.S.V.P.: Number attending:

Gift: Thank you sent:

Guest:

Address:

Phone:

R.S.V.P.: Number attending:

Gift: Thank you sent:

Guests

Guest:

Address:

Phone:

R.S.V.P.: Number attending:

Gift: Thank you sent:

Guest:

Address:

Phone:

R.S.V.P.: Number attending:

Gift: Thank you sent:

Guest:

Address:

Phone:

R.S.V.P.: Number attending:

Gift: Thank you sent:

Guest:

Address:

Phone:

R.S.V.P.: Number attending:

Gift: Thank you sent:

Guest:

Address:

Phone:

R.S.V.P.: Number attending:

Gift: Thank you sent:

RECEPTION

Guests

Guest:

Address:

Phone:

R.S.V.P.: Number attending:

Gift: Thank you sent:

Guest:

Address:

Phone:

R.S.V.P.: Number attending:

Gift: Thank you sent:

Guest:

Address:

Phone:

R.S.V.P.: Number attending:

Gift: Thank you sent:

Guest:

Address:

Phone:

R.S.V.P.: Number attending:

Gift: Thank you sent:

Guest:

Address:

Phone:

R.S.V.P.: Number attending:

Gift: Thank you sent:

Guests

Guest:

Address:

Phone:

R.S.V.P.: Number attending:

Gift: Thank you sent:

Guest:

Address:

Phone:

R.S.V.P.: Number attending:

Gift: Thank you sent:

Guest:

Address:

Phone:

R.S.V.P.: Number attending:

Gift: Thank you sent:

Guest:

Address:

Phone:

R.S.V.P.: Number attending:

Gift: Thank you sent:

Guest:

Address:

Phone:

R.S.V.P.: Number attending:

Gift: Thank you sent:

RECEPTION

Guests

Guest:

Address:

Phone:

R.S.V.P.: Number attending:

Gift: Thank you sent:

Guest:

Address:

Phone:

R.S.V.P.: Number attending:

Gift: Thank you sent:

Guest:

Address:

Phone:

R.S.V.P.: Number attending:

Gift: Thank you sent:

Guest:

Address:

Phone:

R.S.V.P.: Number attending:

Gift: Thank you sent:

Guest:

Address:

Phone:

R.S.V.P.: Number attending:

Gift: Thank you sent:

Guests

Guest:

Address:

Phone:

R.S.V.P.: Number attending:

Gift: Thank you sent:

Guest:

Address:

Phone:

R.S.V.P.: Number attending:

Gift: Thank you sent:

Guest:

Address:

Phone:

R.S.V.P.: Number attending:

Gift: Thank you sent:

Guest:

Address:

Phone:

R.S.V.P.: Number attending:

Gift: Thank you sent:

Guest:

Address:

Phone:

R.S.V.P.: Number attending:

Gift: Thank you sent:

RECEPTION

Guests

Guest:

Address:

Phone:

R.S.V.P.:   Number attending:

Gift: Thank you sent:

Guest:

Address:

Phone:

R.S.V.P.:   Number attending:

Gift: Thank you sent:

Guest:

Address:

Phone:

R.S.V.P.:   Number attending:

Gift: Thank you sent:

Guest:

Address:

Phone:

R.S.V.P.:   Number attending:

Gift: Thank you sent:

Guest:

Address:

Phone:

R.S.V.P.:   Number attending:

Gift: Thank you sent:

BRIDAL
REGISTRY

Faint heart never won fair lady!

Nothing venture, nothing win—

Blood is thick, but water's thin—

In for a penny, in for a pound—

It's Love that makes the world go round!

—SIR WILLIAM SCHWENCK GILBERT, 1861-1911

Gift Registry Summary

Store registered:

Address:

Phone:

Store registered:

Address:

Phone:

Store registered:

Address:

Phone:

Store registered:

Address:

Phone:

Gift Registry

Store registered:

Address:

Phone:

Date registered:

Formal dinnerware pattern:

Silver pattern:

Casual dinnerware pattern:

Casual flatware pattern:

Crystal:

Stemware:

Pieces registered for:

Gift Registry

Store registered: _____

Address: _____

_____

Phone: _____

Date registered: _____

Pieces registered for: _____

_____

_____

_____

_____

_____

_____

_____

_____

_____

_____

_____

_____

_____

_____

_____

Gift Registry

Store registered:

Address:

Phone:

Date registered:

Pieces registered for:

Gift Registry

Store registered:

Address:

Phone:

Date registered:

Pieces registered for:

HONEYMOON

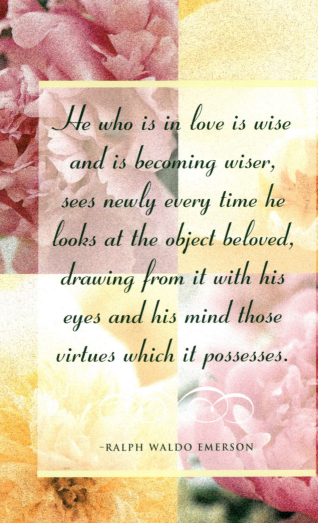

He who is in love is wise and is becoming wiser, sees newly every time he looks at the object beloved, drawing from it with his eyes and his mind those virtues which it possesses.

-RALPH WALDO EMERSON

Honeymoon Wish List

Dream Destinations:

_____

_____

_____

_____

_____

_____

_____

_____

_____

_____

_____

_____

_____

_____

_____

_____

_____

_____

_____

_____

_____

_____

_____

_____

_____

Honeymoon

Destination:

Travel Agency:

Agent's name:

Phone:

Itinerary:

ght Information/Transportation:

commodations:

ntal Car:

ne:

er:

Packing List

NOTES

Flowers have spoken to me more than I can tell in written words. They are the hieroglyphics of angels, loved by all men for the beauty of character, though few can decypher even fragments of their meaning.

—LYDIA M. CHILD,

Notes

Copyright 1997 in all countries of the International Copyright Union by GMG Publishing Corp. All rights reserved.

All flowers and arrangements courtesy of Marilyn & Meredith Waga, Belle Fleur, New York City (212) 688-6371
Photography ©1997 by Michael Grand

A Galison Book
Published by GMG Publishing Corp.
36 West 44th Street, New York, NY 10036
ISBN 1-561557-65-X

Design Director: Heather Zschock
Production Managers: June Lang & Mahin Kooros
Publisher: Gerald Galison

Printed in Hong Kong